THE SWITCH UP!

Cortez Bass
The Switch Up

Published by Spines
ISBN: 979-8-89383-714-8

THE SWITCH UP!

HOW THE OPPORTUNITIES CAME CLEAR

CORTEZ BASS

CONTENTS

CHAPTER 1
THE BEGINNING

Boom! It was the first day of high school. Mom knocked on my door, and I jumped up out of bed, eyes still half-closed and mouth dry as ever—laughing out loud. Anyone who knows the first day of high school knows you have to be stepping just right. I mean fresh shoes, fresh clothes, fresh haircut, etc. So, here it was 6:45 am, and I was rushing to the bathroom to get myself together and head out the door.

As I brushed my teeth, I suddenly turned to my right and caught a strong smell from my right underarm. OMG, was I disappointed! I had to hop in the shower and take a bath again, all while remembering the time because, in high school, no matter what, the bus was never late. I wonder why that was. As I was taking a shower, my mom yelled from the kitchen, "Hurry up and get out of that shower! You are going to miss the bus, and if so, I am not taking you. Better get PAT & CHARLIE ready to walk." Laughing out loud. For those who don't know what that means, it refers to using your left and right foot to walk.

I didn't want to walk, so I rushed out of the shower and into the bedroom, ready to put on my new outfit with my crispy white Air Forces. I was already thinking about what I was going to say when my friends asked me, "Hey, what did you get for school clothes this year?" I already had it written down, waiting for the question.

It's 7:20 am, and the bus is expected to arrive at 7:30 am. I'm walking up the street to the bus, doing the duck walk because I didn't want to crease my new pair of crispy white Air Forces. As I get to the bus stop, I look around at my neighborhood friends. Everyone is clean and looking fresh. About 10 minutes later, we see the bus coming, so we start to make a line to get on the bus.

As I'm walking to the bus, talking to one of my buddies and not looking, I step right into a puddle of water, messing up my shoes. OMG, I was so upset with myself for not paying attention. As I get on the bus, I see my friend Brian. He was a fresh kid from the neighborhood, always with the latest gear and more. I asked Brian, "Hey man, what should I do about my shoes messing up in the puddle?" Of course, Brian had the perfect solution. He reaches into his bag and pulls out a sandwich bag full of solutions and toothbrushes. He says to me, "No worries, I stay prepared for situations like this." As we ride, Brian is cleaning my shoes, and we head to school.

As we pull into the school parking lot, Brian gives me my new clean, crispy white Air Forces, and I proceed off the bus. Now, this is the point where everyone is excited to see what all our friends are wearing and to catch up on summer break talks. As I am walking down the hallway, I see my buddy from childhood. We start to talk in the hallway, comparing ideas about clothes and watching all the beautiful young ladies walk by.

So, my buddy and I head to the lunchroom to grab breakfast. We are in line, and of course, my high school crush walks in and jumps in front of us. I'm just sweating, nervous, and stuck all in one—laughing out loud. I say, "Hey, let me carry your tray to the table," and she looks back and says, "Yes, I would love that." As I proceed to the table, all my buddies are clapping, laughing, and talking to me because, at this point, she has me open. I feel like the whole cafeteria knows I'm all in love.

Suddenly, I look down and wasn't paying attention. When I look up, I bump straight into her, and milk goes everywhere. The expression she gave me was furious. As I look to explain, the first period bell rings, and she storms off. To myself, I say, "WHAT A FIRST DAY OF SCHOOL FOR ME."

CHAPTER 2
WHEN IT ALL CAME CLEAR

So, hey. Here we are, 12th grade of high school, ready to take off to the next level. High school for me was more like a family reunion because my school was basically a lot of friends and family. I had known them for a very long time. We went to elementary school and middle school together, so it was always full of fun and great stories.

My last year of high school taught me a lot of lessons. One of the most important was the need to have a plan after graduation. If you weren't going to college, you would enter the adult world very quickly. After I left high school, I got my first job ever, working at a cleaners in my hometown. It was great. I loved this job and all the people who worked there. This job taught me a lot about discipline, patience with people, and how to treat others so they can treat you the same.

On my first day of work, I was separating the non-starch clothes from the starch clothes when a car pulled up in the drive-thru. "Hello, sir. How are you?" I greeted, but received no response. I continued to be polite and asked, "Are we applying starch to your jeans or shirts?" He replied, "Did I say that?" He was clearly upset. I didn't know what was going on with his day, but I had to make it better so he would treat others how he wanted to be treated. As he gave me his laundry to wash, I gave him a 30% coupon for his next order. His expression was amazing. He thanked me and said, "You are going to be blessed. You never gave up on treating me with respect." From that moment, I learned that you never know what people are going through, so it's always kind to make sure their day is better, especially if you have the ability to do so.

Working at the cleaners had its cons as well because on the other side of the cleaners was a laundromat, so it stayed busy. I mean busy! One day, about 8 p.m. (we closed at 9 p.m.), a lady and her son were just sitting at the back of the laundromat. It was very dark back there, so I asked her, "Hey, are you all waiting for clothes to dry?" She responded, "No." At this point, I was all over the place because this was clean-up hour for me, and I had a customer here. I then asked her, "So can I help you with something?" She told me, "Yes, $5 so we can eat." I learned a long time ago from my family that you never want to see anyone hungry, so I proceeded to give her the $5. As I did so, she took the little boy in her arms and took off through the woods behind the laundromat. "OMG," I said to myself. This was a weird day for me.

As I got older, I started to gain more knowledge about how adult life worked, and I wanted my first car ever. I said to myself, I want an old-school Cutlass, so I knew I had to work hard to get it because my mom lived by the "If you don't work, you don't get" morals. I had a buddy selling a 1987 Cutlass Supreme. OMG, did I want that car so bad. I worked my butt off and finally got my old-school Cutlass. I had so many plans for this car. I used to drive it to work every day. I had put some little cheap subwoofers in the trunk. I mean, I just thought I was it.

One day, my Cutlass was giving me trouble with starting up, so my mom took me to work. Of course, she talked my head off about buying that old car and said I needed to get "Pat & Charlie" (meaning my feet) ready tomorrow if the car didn't crank up. "Laughing out loud." I had mechanics after mechanics come looking at my car, telling me all types of stuff about what it could be (shaking my head).

One day, I decided to go outside myself and see what I could do. I had my little cheap tool bag and gloves on, ready to take on the world because I needed my ride. As I was checking the battery and looking at the belts and everything, I went to start the car up, or at least try. I tried for about 20 minutes to start the car, and as I looked under the hood, it was smoking. "OMG," was I in trouble. I ran around the car and noticed it was on fire. I mean fire! My mom had to call 911.

CHAPTER 3

TAKING ON THE WORLD

This is my first year at my job, and it is going great. My dad gave me an Astro van—an old van, but hey, I was excited about it. My dad had put some 18-inch rims on it and all. "Laughing out loud," I was in the game for sure.

As I was still working at the cleaners, I started hanging out with two of my guy friends from school; we were tight. I remember getting off work one evening when my buddy called me up and said, "Hey, let's hang out when you get off work. There's a party going on, and there are going to be plenty of girls there." So, me being me, that was my weakness. "Laughing out loud," you couldn't tell me anything about a lady or anything because I was all there.

It's 8:45 p.m., and we are closing up the cleaners. I'm super hyped about the night. I'm headed straight home and putting on my new pair of Coogi jeans, shirt, and fresh pair of all-white Air Force 1 Nikes. As I'm riding, having the radio pumped up loud, listening to some good old hip-hop, just vibing in my own zone, ready to take on the night with the fellas, I get a call from one of my buddies. He's like, "Hey, can we come over to your place, get dressed, and pregame?"

At this point, I'm confused because I'm like, "Y'all for sure can get dressed here, but what does the pregame include?" So I'm like, "Yes, that's cool. I'll be there in a second; just wait for me outside." After I pull up, I run straight past my mom to the bedroom, pulling out my outfit, getting it squared away. While waiting for my buddies to come over, I practice my talk game in the mirror, thinking about what I was going to say when a nice young lady walked by. "Laughing out loud."

As I'm putting on my clothes, I hear a knock on the door, so I run straight to it—my buddies have arrived. As they walk in, I hear one of them say, "Cortez, are you ready for the pregame?" Now I'm all ears; I have to find out what this pregame is about. So I'm like, "HEY, what's the pregame consist of?" One of my buddies pulls out of his bookbag a colorful wrapped candy bar and a handful of grass. He says, "We are going to smoke some weed tonight to mellow us out."

So, my eyes get big, and I'm like, "Hey, let's go outside and let me see what that's about." Growing up around a lot of my older family, I had smelled it before but never tried it myself. As we are outside, I ask my buddies, "Hey, have you guys done this before?" They both look at me and say, "Yes, all the time. It just keeps you mellow, and you will have fun, believe me." So here I am, smoking. After about two hits, I feel myself going into a daze. "OMG, tonight is going to be wild," I say to myself.

We are dressed and ready to go out tonight. My buddy is driving, and I'm in the back seat, watching all the cars pass by and all the lights. I'm stuck at this point, very mellowed out. "Laughing out loud." We pull up to the party. The line is very long, but we have VIP tickets to get in, so we are going straight in. The crowd is major thick inside—so many people dancing and having a great time. My buddies and I head straight to the restroom to check our fits and talk about the ladies we saw coming in. "Laughing out loud."

As I look in the mirror at myself, I see that my mouth looks white and my eyes are bloodshot red. I immediately get nervous. "OMG." As we head back out, there's a group of ladies standing by the door. I'm so nervous; I hear one of them speak, but I hope they can't see my eyes, so I quickly turn and say, "Hey, do you smoke weed?" "OMG," did her eyes light up. I was just asking the first thing that came to my mind. She immediately answered, "Yes, all the time. This must be your first time." Quickly again, I'm like, "Nah, I do this all the time."

"Laughing out loud." I didn't want to be singled out for sure.

As we are conversing, my buddies are on the dance floor, grooving to the music. This nice-looking female and I are standing all alone in the corner. Maybe she felt mellow and was just grooving to the music. At the end of the party, my buddies were ready to go. I ask the nice lady, "Hey, can we hang out sometime, maybe grab some food?" I was so locked in, I felt like I should grab her number. She replied, "Yes, sure, take my number."

As I'm walking out of the party, my chest is stuck out. I'm feeling myself now, ready to ask the fellas how they did with girls at the party.

As we get in the car, I tell my buddy, "Hey, I still smell weed in the vehicle. Do we have more?" I was just asking because I felt like it was sitting beside me in the car in the back seat with the seatbelt on, laughing out loud. So my buddy said to me, "Yes, I have a small amount left on me."

As we are driving close to my area where I stay, a police car gets behind us with their lights on. "OMG," I said to myself. This can't be how the night ends! At this point, I'm nervous and thinking about all the things I'm going to lose and how my mom is going to tell me about all the things I could have done to avoid this. SMH.

As the officer walks up, he asks for license and registration from my buddy and then walks back to his car. As the officer is running everything, we are all quiet and nervous. We try to talk each other through what could happen and what we could have done differently. When the officer comes back to the car, he says, "Hey, slow down and you all get home safe." OMG, did our hearts drop!

Growing up around my city, there were a lot of police on patrol after every party because it was a city of crime and late-night partying due to all the colleges nearby. As we get to dropping me off at home, my buddy asks me before I get out, "Hey, do you want to smoke before you go in?" I give him this look like, "If you don't go home, you better," laughing out loud.

I continue to go in the house. My mom is up because she was that type of parent. Knowing the city we lived in, she usually waited up until we got home safe. Usually, I sit up with my mom and tell her about my nights, but tonight I was so nervous I felt she already knew. SMH. She asked me, "Hey, Cortez, anything exciting happen tonight?" My eyes lit up like a deer's. I proceed to her and say, "Yes, I got a pretty lady's number and we are going to hang out soon." She looked me up and down with a smirk like, "Yeah, okay."

I walked to my bedroom, and just as I'm about to lay down, she bursts into my room and says, "Hey, I saw you guys got pulled over after the party." I immediately jumped up. OMG, how did she know? Well, my mom was that type of concerned parent, or maybe she was just nosey, lol, but either way, she must have driven by the party. So I say to her, "Yes, it was just a traffic stop. Nothing serious." My mom gave me that look again like, "Boy, okay."

I kept a good relationship with my mom. She kind of always knew what I was doing and when I was doing it, but I still don't know how, lol. As I was still learning new things in the world, I met my first girlfriend. OMG, was this a story. We were just alike. Everything I was thinking about, she was thinking about. It was crazy. But coming from my city, there were plenty of girls, but a lot of them were addicted to the popular crowd and guys. Me, I was not the one. I learned early I never wanted to be in big crowds because that's where a lot of miscommunication and drama come from, so I pretty much stayed to myself. But I did know a lot of people, just that they were cool.

So my new girlfriend and I started kicking it real good. I used to spend the night at her house, but my mom never liked that. My mom grew up in that era where guys and girls don't sleep over until they are grown. Well, I considered myself grown, especially after I met my girlfriend. Her mom loved me sleeping over, and I stayed there all week, mostly going to work and back to my girlfriend's place. It got so bad my mom used to tell me, "You might as well change your address to over there," lol. I really think she was missing me.

One afternoon, I get a call from my girlfriend, and she is

all over the place telling me to get off work ASAP. I need to come over right now. See, I stayed working a lot because I loved things, and the things I wanted were costly. So I get off work and head towards her house. As soon as I walk in, she has a blank stare. OMG, what is wrong now? She says to me, "Cortez, I'm pregnant. I've done three tests and all came back positive." My eyes were so big. All I could do was drop to my knees and think, "I'm having my first child, and I am not prepared!"

CHAPTER 4
THE START OVER!

So let's go back to the beginning, when I started to figure things out slowly but surely. I grew up in an era where it was really fend for yourself. It was crazy, but it was just the generation we grew up in.

With that being said, when I was younger, my grandad was a very special person. He stayed busy, and I loved to be around him all the time. But I had a cousin also; he was with him 24/7. I used to not understand that, but over time I realized it was a fend for yourself type of deal. If I wasn't prepared to go with my grandad, I was going to be left behind every time, no matter what.

My grandma and grandad stayed close to me, so I decided if I was going to be like my cousin and hang out with grandad all the time, I had to get on my bike and fly down to my grandparents' house. It used to be crazy between me and my cousin because we used to argue about who was sitting in the middle or who was sitting by the window. My grandad had a little pickup truck, so it was tight in there.

In 2005, my grandad passed away, and it really took a toll on everyone in the family, especially me because he was like a role model. I loved him for always showing me how to be an entrepreneur from the beginning. My grandma was so sweet; she kept the family together until she passed away years later. After that, it was crazy for the family. It seemed everyone had split up, and it was never the same for birthdays or holidays.

As I got older, I realized you have to always keep yourself in peaceful situations to get through anything in life, no matter what. So as I was getting older, I started to hang more in the streets and with my buddies. But where I come from, there was always something going on in the neighborhood or in the area. We were selling drugs, smoking, drinking, and everything else. It was hard for us in my city, so we had to make a way to make money and survive.

At this point, I had my first baby, and my child's mom and I were living together, so I had to make sure we had financial stability. In the generation I grew up in, our schools didn't teach us how to become entrepreneurs and start our own companies. All we knew in my family was to go to work, and I knew I didn't like work because I hated the manager telling me to do this or clock out here, etc. So I kind of knew back in my age that I would be an entrepreneur, or at least I was praying one day I'd be working for myself like my grandad and controlling my own destiny.

One day, I was hanging with my buddies around the house when we heard a loud bang on the door. Of course, we were doing our thing, not thinking about the trouble it could bring. When we answered the door, it was the local authorities. We all went downtown in handcuffs, and from that day, I said to myself I wanted to find a different avenue of work, be successful in it, and never look back on what I had been through. I also wanted to show my son a different avenue instead of what we see on TV or in music videos.

As I was thinking of another avenue to start my business and entrepreneurial journey, I kept running into dead-end jobs because my mentality was too strong to just be an employee. I used to be at work, and when they told me to do a project, I would go and tell another employee to do it like I was the boss (laughing out loud). So I knew it wouldn't be long before they would let me go!

At one time, I started working at a supermarket and a parts store at the same time. I was okay with doing that because I knew to overcome obstacles in business, you have to be prepared. So I kept working both jobs, and it was fine until one evening when my buddies and I went out on the town. We were having a great time until we were leaving, and a great night turned into a bad situation. We were all very surprised. It seemed to me I just needed to be away from my comfort zone because it seemed I was staying in something that was not good for me or the journey I wanted to reach.

CHAPTER 5
LETTING EVERYTHING RUN ITS COURSE!

Learning from my last situation, I told myself I had two options: I was going to end up in jail or end up dead. So, I had to make a better decision for myself and my son. I went out and got a job working on the money truck. This job was a whole different type of work that I wasn't used to, but it was a pie job. It taught me valuable lessons and showed me a lot of money. (WOOHOO!) Was I excited!

As I was working on the money truck, I started to realize I was really growing within myself. I had my first kid, and it was a great life. While working in that field, I learned how to defend myself and also how to carry and use a firearm. One evening, I had a big turn in my life—a situation that could have taken me away from my family and kid. It was the worst thing I had encountered and brought me serious nightmares.

As I was figuring everything out, I focused on how I could leave my comfort zone and start a new life because I really wanted to better myself. So, I ended up signing up for truck driving school in Missouri. It was my first big experience being away from my family. Some of them were on board, and some were telling me, "No, don't leave; it's dangerous out there, and no real money is made." But I decided to take my own chance and see for myself. I left in 2015.

The journey to my trucking school was hell (LOL). Riding the Greyhound bus, stopping multiple times, trying to sleep—OMG—and of course, I snored, so I was waking up every five minutes looking around like, "Did anyone hear me?" {LOL}. Well, here we are in Missouri, ready to start my new journey and try to meet new friends so I could get the process done smoothly.

As we were in orientation, I met a couple of people that I had met on the bus coming to the school. While talking in class, I met my buddy J. He was from NC also, so we connected so well. We laughed and talked about the ride there and how the free lunch they fed us was not what we were used to {LOL}. Class was going well. I tested out for my permit and failed my first time {OMG}. I was furious. I had studied, I thought, my hardest, but I had to call home to my mom for more inspiration. Of course, she gave me the speech to never give up and keep fighting.

As I headed back to my hotel room that I shared with my buddy from NC, I told him, and while he was waiting to test out, we studied together to make it a little bit easier. We stayed up all night quizzing each other and all. Well, the next day came, and we both headed to the DMV to test out. I was shaking the whole way there, just trying to focus on what my mom had told me and also the words my buddy and I studied together. We walked into the DMV, pumped. I headed to the first computer, sat down, hands sweaty and eyes wide open. I took the test, and at the end, a big green "passed" sign came up. I was so happy. I fell to my knees and was so grateful.

I called home and told everyone. I called my girlfriend at the time, and she said, "I also have great news: I'm pregnant!"

CHAPTER 6

JUMPING INTO IT!

5 AM alarm is going off. This was my first load since I got my CDL and my own truck. So, this load was straight out of Missouri, where I tested, so I didn't have far to drive. Waking up and having to think about how I have a baby on the way and I'm hundreds of miles away was tough for me and my child's mom.

As I'm getting loaded, the loader tells me to pull up; I was too far back, I guess all the stuff going on in my head had me all over the place. So, I finished getting loaded and started to get myself situated for this long ride to California. It was my first time alone, and boy was I excited to see the other side of the world by myself.

One thing I learned about driving trucks is that it gives you a lot of time to think on your own and a lot of peaceful times. I used to come up with crazy ideas and couldn't wait to tell my boys; they'd be like, "Yeah, you've got too much time on your hands" (lol). But they used to also tell me all the time that the stuff I come up with is the best game plan when you're all alone and at peace.

So here we are, riding to California. I'm halfway through the trip and I remembered, "Hey, I have to do my mandatory 30-minute break." So, I pull over to a Flying J travel stop in Albuquerque, where my trainer and I used to stop all the time. They had a taco truck and also a strip club across from the truck stop (lol). Wait, wait, don't get so happy; this was a strip club where you can only see them through the windows, smh.

As I'm pulling in, I see the taco guy's lights on. I ran fast to the truck to grab me a couple of tacos and yes, of course, loaded (LOL). As I'm eating, I'm watching my clock count down; 5 more minutes left in my break, so I'm getting ready to pull off. I push the brakes in, yes, we are back to the open road, turn my music up, listening to my Pandora, just enjoying this ride.

So, a buddy of mine calls, we are talking about how his truck is doing and where he is going. As a trucker, I had to realize real quick you have to have your morning drivers and your mid and nighttime drivers to call because every shift is different.

So, as we are laughing and talking, my stomach starts to talk to me. I immediately look for the nearest truck stop or rest area, but of course, on I-40, the stops were far apart from each other. I turned all the music off and AC off. So, I come to this one big hill, and the sign says test area 50 miles. I immediately pull over with my bag and wipes, and next was self, not what I expected!

CHAPTER 7
LEARNING DIFFERENT OBSTACLES

Here we are, I have my first load and California is my destination. I always was interested in how companies decided on how they wanted to move their freight. So, soon I started to watch a lot of videos on trucking and how freight moved across the world. Driving trucks was a peaceful thing to me, even though I was missing family and friends at home. I used to get this sensation that brought me to always enjoy cranking up my truck and getting my load details, enjoying the open road.

Back to me rolling down the highway, I have 6 months in, no accidents, and no late arrivals. (Ring, Ring) My dispatch is calling me. "Hey Cortez, I have a great opportunity for you I think you will love." So, me, I loved new opportunities; it brought smiles to me. So my dispatch says, "How would you like to be a trainer?" Immediately, I started to smile; my heart got so warm. So I'm just thinking, why me? I just started driving. So I tell him, "Yes, I would love to train students." He tells me I'm going to reroute you back in to get you scheduled for training class for 3 days and we are going to get you connected with a student right away. So I'm super excited. I'm calling all of my family and friends; this is a new obstacle for me and I cannot fail on this opportunity.

Here we go, first day with my student. His name was Roy; he was from Maryland, an older guy. He was very interested at first until I started to inform him of my truck rules. He felt like I was being rude because I told him shoes were not to be worn in the back of the bunk area. That was because when you wear your shoes out of the truck, you may be stepping in everything outside. He was like, "This is a work truck, not a home." I had told him numerous times, "This is my home away from home." I quickly realized a lot of older folks never want to be told what to do from a younger person, I guess because of the age difference.

So we are 3 weeks in and my student tells me, "Hey, I want a different trainer. I feel this is not going to be a good fit." So of course, I granted his wishes and called my dispatch and he routed us back in. As soon as I get back to the terminal, my dispatch meets us outside and tells me, "Cortez, I have a different type of student for you. This student is an older female from Georgia, never drove before but is very eager to get rolling." So I gave the student a call and we loaded the truck up and got to rolling.

Well, this lady was a great connection. She listened and was very respectful to my truck. First dispatch, we are headed to California. We drop the load; student is doing excellent, no problems, smooth. Next load, we are headed to Oregon, so we have a good long ride from the bottom of California to the top of California. So while we are riding, my student reminds me she has home time coming up and she needs to be home soon. So I tell dispatch and he is already working us a load from Oregon to Georgia. We drop in Oregon, pick up a preload from Oregon headed to Georgia. Well, I was one of those trainers who wanted my student to get some night driving while I sleep and get some good experience.

Here we are, loaded with potatoes coming through Utah around 11 p.m. I hear my student SCREAMING at the top of her lungs, "CORTEZ!" I immediately jump up and look, and we are at the top of a mountain, blizzard and all. OMG, was I nervous! My student was freaking out, and we had no option but to get down the mountain. So I immediately tell her, "Calm down, let's take it slow." She says to me, "I'm ready to go home; this is my last load. This is not a part of the world." So in my mind, I realized this was my last student because I really was putting my life in their hands. So I took over the driver's seat, and we proceeded down the hill and continued our journey. But on the way to her destination, she was telling me that where we were is not a real place no matter what and she doesn't want to see that ever again.

But in my mind, I'm thinking, yes, OTR trucking might not be for you because that comes with being OTR and running into different situations and obstacles. Here we are in Georgia, and she proceeds off the truck, and my dispatch calls and says let's try to get another student immediately. I tell him, "No way, I'm going to continue with being solo." He falls out laughing, and now I'm back to the open road in my peaceful zone!

CHAPTER 8

PUTTING KNOWLEDGE TO PLAY

Trucking was always fun to me. I loved it and still do, but I was so interested in the movement of the freight that I had to find out more. So here I am, three years in at my first company, and I decided to take my knowledge to another company in Oklahoma. I liked the trucks they had and they were offering more, so I moved companies.

While I was there, I started to get more information with the dispatch services while I was working. I also used my trucker knowledge from the last company to put me in a better position at this new company. One day, I asked the dispatch, "How do you all get paid and what lanes do you run depending on the drivers you hire?" He immediately asked me, "Why are you so interested?"

I came to the conclusion that the part of trucking I was interested in was kind of the bug part of how logistics of the trucking industry was run, and they didn't want me to find out. So I stayed with that company about one and a half years because of one thing: my loads were not equaling up to my pay that I was promised, so I decided to go back to my original company and do more of my research.

Of course, when I came back, they were determined to put me back into the training game. I took it, but I took it for other reasons. That was to see and research all I could of how the logistics and freight moved around the country. I became one of the top trainers of my team, and I was super excited. I used the knowledge that I knew and learned and started going out on the pad and helping other drivers with students, showing them a different way so the students could understand the concept a lot better.

Here we are. I have got a student that was brand new – I mean no CDL permit or anything; he was starting from the bottom. So I had to help him study the CDL book so he could first grab his permit. I had a method I had learned, and it was everything that I had underneath the hood of the truck was "not bent, broken, cracked," and everything soft underneath the hood had "no abrasions, bulges, cuts." He learned that, and after two days of studying, he passed the test on his first day. Boy, was I super hyped!

The next step for him was to drive his hours and pass the CDL road test. In Missouri, the test was hard, and they were very strict, so I knew I had to take my time and show him the right way. We were practicing for his test tomorrow, and he was very nervous. I told him, "Just take your time, and remember when backing up, never oversteer."

The alarm goes off. It's Monday, 5 in the morning, and the test is about to start. We go to the pad, and my student is number four to test out. He is extra nervous because he saw the first couple of students fail. I had to remind him, "Just pretend they are not watching you and continue to be great." He proceeds to the pad to grab the truck and starts his test.

He is passing the first part, and now he is heading to the road to do the driving part of the test. About 30 minutes later, I see the truck coming back in. I am super nervous myself now. The CDL Examiner comes to me and says, "He passed everything, Cortez. You did an amazing job." My student hears him and immediately drops to his knees, thanking me. This was a blessing because I had really changed someone's livelihood for the better.

My dispatch calls me and says he'll meet me by the cafeteria. I go over, but I just knew he is going to tell me some bad news. I see him there with the owner of the company and a plaque in his hand. He says, "We want to reward you with the Trainer Award of the Year!"

OMG, my life has turned, and my knowledge is paying off!

CHAPTER 9
CONTINUING TO BE AN ASSET

Here I am, 7 years in the trucking industry. I have trained over 5 students, and I was super proud about this. So while I was working with my same company I started with, I had figured out a lot about how freight moved and how dispatch was a main feature in the industry. So I decided I wanted to come off of the road and continue my journey in being local and opening my own dispatch service to accommodate other companies and to give them great service.

So it's the year of 2022, and I'm local. Me and my uncle open up our own trucking company, and we are rolling, learning new things as we go. Also, I am learning how to run a company efficiently and set up new business opportunities that will help me with other entrepreneurs who are interested in getting into the industry. So I thought to myself, I think I wanted to continue my grandparents' legacy and open a cleaning business to help some local companies with some quality cleaning. And I did exactly what I said I was going to do.

I was cleaning all around NC, and I had a team. They were always down to grow and to gain more clients. OMG, were we rolling! Until one day, I had to clean a building due to a cleaner calling out, but also I had to drive my truck to get a load. That day taught me a lot about being an owner of your own company. You had to play all positions no matter what because you were the face of the company. So I did exactly that. I cleaned that building and with little sleep, also made it my duty to grab that load to continue growing our trucking company.

Well, one day I said to myself I'm going to turn this janitorial company over and continue to open a logistics company to leverage the trucking we were doing. So I exactly did that. I handed it over to my Charlotte team, and the workers were so grateful. After a couple of months, me and a buddy of mine came together and opened a local logistics company. We ran a couple of our local friends' and family's trucks to help them bring in good revenue and also learn the industry on the way up.

One year in, I said to myself I wanted to start to teach people this talent and offer a great dispatch service around the world. Not just call yourself a dispatch and offer immaculate service!

CHAPTER 10
WHERE THE OPPURTUNITIES CAME CLEAR!

In 2023, at 8 am in my office, I had started to write up a packet, going step by step on how to learn to be a great dispatcher. I wrote it to the "T" – nothing was left out. So, I kept the packet enclosed and just held onto it for knowledge until one day, my buddy said, "Man, I want to learn about the logistics of trucking but I don't want to go to school."

I remembered I had a packet that I had written up and thought it could be helpful to him. So, I gave him the packet, and after a week, he came to me saying, "Cortez, this is a book you have written and you don't even know it." Of course, I initially thought, "Yeah, nobody is going to read that." Until one day, I said, "Let's try and see where it goes."

I went to Staples – lol – and did a test run on my step-by-step book. I got them to print me a couple of copies to see who would love this information. When I posted it on a couple of social media platforms, people were like, "Hey, how can I get a couple?" I was so shocked about this. I said to myself, "I have to reach out to an agency. This is too much to be distributing books myself. It was just a lot."

So, in June 2023, my agency got a hold of the book, and in August 2023, my book was released. It was doing great in the industry – people really wanted to learn this knowledge. From there, I learned, "If you open someone's eyes to something, you can definitely bring them in." I also realized that no matter if you think it's not good enough for you, it might be the best insight for someone else chasing a dream and could change their life forever.

As my book was selling all over the internet, I was getting booked for seminars to start teaching other companies and entrepreneurs how to leverage their companies. This was a big blessing to me – to help others see the other side of trucking. So here we are now, in 2024, and book sales are still going strong. People are still booking me for seminars and learning from my step-by-step guide, "Learning the Trucking Industry."

I just want to remind everyone: once you see a vision in your eyesight or dreams, make sure you chase them and never give up. I'm Cortez Bass, and now the journey continues after my switch up!

www.ingramcontent.com/pod-product-compliance
Lightning Source LLC
Chambersburg PA
CBHW021149130726
47988CB00004B/1535